THOMAS JEFFERSON'S

★ PRESIDENCY ★

Presidential Powerhouses

THOMAS JEFFERSON'S
★ PRESIDENCY ★

EMILY ROSE OACHS

LERNER PUBLICATIONS ◆ MINNEAPOLIS

Lerner Publications Company
A division of Lerner Publishing Group, Inc.
241 First Avenue North
Minneapolis, MN 55401 USA

For reading levels and more information, look up this title at
www.lernerbooks.com.

Main body text set in Caecilia LT Std 9.5/15.
Typeface provided by Adobe Systems.

Library of Congress Cataloging-in-Publication Data

Oachs, Emily Rose.
     Thomas Jefferson's presidency / by Emily Rose Oachs.
        pages cm. — (Presidential powerhouses)
     ISBN 978-1-4677-7923-4 (lb : alk. paper)
     ISBN 978-1-4677-8602-7 (eb pdf)
     1. Jefferson, Thomas, 1743–1826—Juvenile literature. 2. United
States—Politics and government—1801–1809—Juvenile literature.
3. Presidents—United States—Biography—Juvenile literature.
I. Title.
E331.O15 2015
973.4'6092—dc23 [B]   2015000549

Manufactured in the United States of America
1-37514-18659-2/24/2016

★ TABLE OF CONTENTS ★

★ INTRODUCTION ★

Nearly a thousand people gathered in the nation's new capital city, Washington, DC, on March 4, 1801, to witness the inauguration of the third president of the United States. The crowd packed into the Senate Chamber of the unfinished Capitol Building. The room was so full, "not another creature could enter," according to writer Margaret Bayard Smith, who attended the event. Seated on the podium was the president-elect Thomas Jefferson. On either side of him sat the Supreme Court chief justice, John Marshall, and the vice president–elect Aaron Burr.

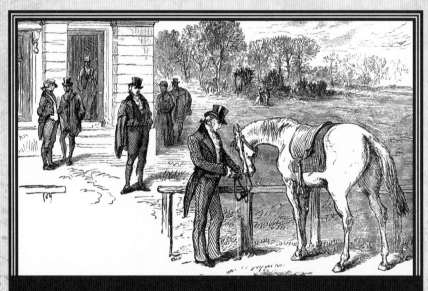

Jefferson arrived in Washington, DC, on horseback, though he walked to the site of his inauguration.

Jefferson had walked with friends through the mild spring air to the Capitol from his nearby boardinghouse. Isaac Jefferson, an enslaved African American man Jefferson owned, described the future president as "a tall, straight-bodied man as ever you see, right square-shouldered. Nary a man in this town walked so straight." But apart from his commanding presence, Jefferson would not have stood out from the crowd on his inauguration day. He wore a simple suit, in contrast to the ceremonial dress of the two previous presidents on their inauguration days. Both George Washington and John Adams had worn stylish suits with a sword at the hip. They had arrived in elegant horse-drawn carriages, while Jefferson had come on foot.

The Capitol grew quiet as Jefferson rose from his seat to speak. Despite the silence, audience members seated behind the first few rows had to strain to hear Jefferson's timid voice, so faint it was almost a whisper. He had printed the speech, however, so those in attendance could choose to read along. Jefferson was a far better writer than orator, and on this day, his lackluster delivery was at odds with the magnitude of his words. Luckily, Americans could read his words later, when a Washington, DC, newspaper, the *National Intelligencer*, reprinted a president's inaugural address for the first time.

Just as the country's capital city was still under construction, so was its national government. The American Revolutionary War (1775–1783) had established a democracy in a world where most rulers inherited or seized their power. Americans were still debating how their democracy should work. Adams and the Federalist Party favored a central government that wielded great power. Jefferson and the Democratic-Republican Party envisioned a limited national government, with individuals and state governments holding most of the power.

The presidential contest between Adams and Jefferson had been so intense and angry that it had threatened the peaceful transfer of power. When Adams lost the election, some Americans, including Virginia governor and ardent Democratic-Republican James Monroe, feared the Federalists might seize control illegally.

In his speech, the new president aimed to calm these fears and to remind Americans that they shared basic principles of government, no matter which political party they supported. Their fierce arguments, Jefferson said, were the sign of a people whose constitution protected their right to think, speak, and write freely. The people had chosen a new president, under the rule of law. "We are all republicans. We are all federalists," Jefferson said. "Let us, then, fellow-citizens, unite with one heart and one mind."

Jefferson stressed in his speech the ideal he had written into the Declaration of Independence twenty-five years earlier, in 1776—that all men are created equal. The US Constitution, he said, would ensure that tolerance and reason prevailed and that people who held a minority point of view would not be silenced or stripped of rights. "All . . . will bear in mind this sacred principle," he stated, "that though the will of the majority is in all cases to prevail, that will to be rightful must be reasonable; that the minority possess their equal rights, which equal law must protect, and to violate would be oppression."

Thomas Jefferson's words reflected his vision of a democratic society. A good government, the new president said, "shall restrain men from injuring one another, shall leave them otherwise free to regulate their own pursuits of industry and improvement, and shall not take from the mouth of labor the bread it has earned."

Isaac Jefferson, also known as Isaac Granger, was one of Jefferson's slaves and a skilled tinsmith and blacksmith.

In his life, however, Jefferson's actions did not always match his ideals. The man who championed self-rule enslaved hundreds of African Americans. As president, Jefferson would also sometimes follow what he considered the most practical course of action, even when it conflicted with his beliefs. Jefferson's ideals and contradictions would color his presidency and his legacy and transform the United States itself.

★ CHAPTER ONE ★

THE VIRGINIAN

Thomas Jefferson was born on April 13, 1743, in Albemarle County in Virginia, the first of the thirteen British colonies. These colonies would become the United States. Thomas was the third of ten children—and the eldest son—of Peter Jefferson and Jane Randolph Jefferson. Jane Jefferson had been born in London, England, but her family immigrated to Virginia when she was a child. Peter Jefferson was a self-educated plantation owner, surveyor, and slaveholder.

Europeans had brought the first enslaved Africans to the colonies in 1619, to Virginia. According to family legend, Thomas Jefferson's first memory was of being carried on a pillow by one of his family's slaves from Shadwell, the plantation where he had been born, to the family's new home at nearby Tuckahoe Plantation.

EDUCATION

Thomas, like many children of his social class, began his schooling with a tutor at home. At the age of nine, he began boarding at a school run by William Douglas, a local Christian clergyman and teacher. Thomas studied the classical languages Latin and Greek, which was typical for a well-educated man

Thomas was born at Shadwell, a plantation in Virginia. This illustration shows the mill and farmhouse at Shadwell.

of his time. When he was fourteen, his beloved father died. The future president then started taking lessons from another clergyman, James Maury, an old friend of his father, who provided Thomas with further education in the classics. Thomas found Maury's religious views too narrow, however.

In March 1760, Jefferson moved to Williamsburg, then the capital of Virginia, to study in the philosophy department of the College of William & Mary. He also studied natural philosophy, as the study of science was then called, and the study of natural phenomenon would become a lifelong love. Almost seventeen years old, Jefferson enjoyed socializing, but he was a diligent student. Awake from dawn until two o'clock in the morning, he studied fifteen hours a day, practiced his violin for three, and slept and took meals during the other six. His friend John Page said that Jefferson "could tear himself away from his dearest friends, to fly to his studies."

Jefferson graduated from college in two years and began studying law under George Wythe, a distinguished lawyer who introduced Jefferson to other leaders of the colony. After almost five years of studying with Wythe, Jefferson was admitted to the bar to practice law in 1767.

A YOUNG STATESMAN

In 1768 Virginians elected twenty-five-year-old Thomas Jefferson to serve in the colony's legislature, the House of Burgesses. Jefferson put his writing talents to work by drafting resolutions and laws for the colony. He associated with fellow legislators George Washington, Patrick Henry, and other like-minded men who opposed the rule the royal governor placed on them. Tensions were rising in the colonies over British-imposed taxation, which upset many colonists because the colonies had no representation in the British Parliament. Jefferson helped

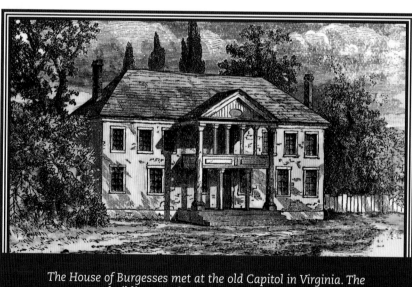

The House of Burgesses met at the old Capitol in Virginia. The building was later destroyed by a fire.

organize protests against British policies that he saw as unjust.

Meanwhile, the young legislator began designing a house to be built on land his father had left him. The property was on a mountaintop across the river from Jefferson's birthplace, so he named the estate Monticello, meaning "little mountain" in Italian. He relied on slaves to farm tobacco and other crops on his 5,000-acre (2,023-hectare) plantation. Slaves also helped construct the house and outbuildings and eventually even made nails and bricks in Monticello's workshops.

On January 1, 1772, Jefferson married young widow Martha Wayles Skelton, who came from a wealthy, prominent family of planters. She and Jefferson shared a love of music. He played the violin, and she played the harpsichord. John Wayles, Jefferson's father-in-law, died in 1773 and left his daughter extensive amounts of property. By law, a married woman's property belonged to her husband. Besides the land, Thomas Jefferson gained possession of 135 slaves, one of the colony's largest holdings of slaves. Among them were Elizabeth Hemings and her children. John Wayles was widely believed to be the father of several of Hemings's children, making these children the enslaved half siblings of Thomas Jefferson's wife, Martha.

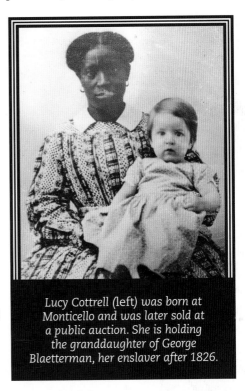

Lucy Cottrell (left) was born at Monticello and was later sold at a public auction. She is holding the granddaughter of George Blaetterman, her enslaver after 1826.

This was possible because white owners were legally free to take sexual advantage of their slaves, with or without the enslaved person's consent. Further, by Virginia law, children born to an enslaved mother were also slaves, even if their fathers were white.

Even as he oversaw the growth of his plantation, Jefferson became increasingly active in politics. In 1774 representatives from each of the colonies gathered to plan resistance to British rule. Jefferson wrote instructions for the delegates who were to attend the nation's First Continental Congress. On his way to present the document to the delegates himself, he became ill. Instead, he sent his slave to deliver it to Patrick Henry. Jefferson's written statement about colonial freedom was later published as the pamphlet *A Summary View of the Rights of British America.*

King George III fought to keep the American colonies under British rule.

Jefferson's argument that it was illegal for King George III of Great Britain to control colonial politics gained him recognition as a patriot leader.

In 1775 Thomas Jefferson was selected as a delegate to the Second Continental Congress. Weeks before the Congress was to meet in Philadelphia, Pennsylvania, British soldiers clashed with colonial militiamen at Lexington and Concord, Massachusetts. In response to the violence, the Continental Congress named George Washington the leader of a newly formed Continental

Army and sent him to take command of the troops. The disputes between Great Britain and its American colonies had flared into war.

THE DECLARATION OF INDEPENDENCE

Jefferson returned to the Continental Congress in May 1776. In June the Congress assigned him to a committee to write a document declaring the colonies' independence from Great Britain. Jefferson's fellow committee members—Benjamin Franklin, Robert Livingston, John Adams, and Roger Sherman— recognized what Adams called Jefferson's "happy talent for composition and singular felicity of expression" and persuaded Jefferson to write the first version.

Left to right, *Benjamin Franklin, John Adams, and Thomas Jefferson meet to review a draft of the Declaration of Independence.*

Jefferson's draft built on European philosophy regarding humans' natural rights, including the right to rebel against an unjust government. He detailed a list of grievances against George III, including the king's failure to protect the colonies from the British Parliament's taxation. In response, the colonies were dissolving their union with Great Britain and establishing an independent new nation—the United States of America.

After incorporating suggestions from Franklin and Adams, Jefferson submitted the declaration to Congress on June 28. The rest of the delegates then edited the document, making several changes and cuts. In one controversial section of the draft, Jefferson blamed King George III for the presence of slavery and the slave trade in the colonies. Though he was a slave owner himself, Jefferson saw slavery as a threat to the security and success of the young United States, and he hoped to

The five-man drafting committee of the Declaration of Independence submits the document to Congress. Jefferson stands in the center in a red vest.

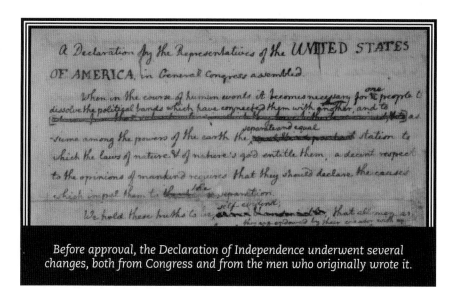

Before approval, the Declaration of Independence underwent several changes, both from Congress and from the men who originally wrote it.

eliminate it from the new nation. To appease Jefferson's fellow slaveholders, Congress edited Jefferson's antislavery language out of the document.

Congress did not, however, alter the stirring words of Jefferson's preamble: "We hold these truths to be self-evident: that all men are created equal; that they are endowed by their creator with certain unalienable Rights; that among these are Life, Liberty and the pursuit of Happiness." Congress ratified the revised Declaration of Independence on July 4, 1776.

That fall Jefferson returned to a legislative position in Williamsburg. Congress had offered him an opportunity to represent the United States in Paris, France, but his wife's ill health prompted him to turn it down. In the legislature, Jefferson met James Madison. Eight years Jefferson's junior, Madison grew to be among Jefferson's closest friends and most trusted political allies.

Around this time, Jefferson took a public stand on the issue of religious freedom. Since 1607 the Episcopal Church, which had its roots in the Church of England, had been the official church

of Virginia, receiving government funds and special treatment over other branches of Christianity. Jefferson advocated freedom of belief and the separation of church and state, meaning that the government should not force Americans to support any religion or use taxpayer money to support churches or clergy. To promote these views, in 1777 Jefferson drafted the Virginia Statute for Religious Freedom. In it he proposed that "no man shall be compelled to frequent or support any religious worship, place, or ministry whatsoever, . . . all men shall be free to profess, and by argument to maintain, their opinions in matters of religion." Jefferson was so proud of authoring the statute that he later wanted the accomplishment noted on his gravestone. The Virginia legislature would pass the statute into law in 1786.

Jefferson also wrote a bill to outlaw the slave trade in Virginia. He called slavery a "hideous blot." In 1778 the state became the

The Jamestown Church is one of the several colonial-era churches from the Church of England that remain in Virginia.

> R UN away from the fubfcriber in *Albemarle,* a Mulatto flave called *Sandy,* about 35 years of age, his ftature is rather low, inclining to corpulence, and his complexion light; he is a fhoemaker by trade, in which he ufes his left hand principally, can do coarfe carpenters work, and is fomething of a horfe jockey; he is greatly addicted to drink, and when drunk is info-lent and diforderly, in his converfation he fwears much, and in his behaviour is artful and knavifh. He took with him a white horfe, much fcarred with traces, of which it is ex-pected he will endeavour to difpofe; he alfo carried his fhoe-makers tools, and will probably endeavour to get employment that way. Whoever conveys the faid flave to me, in *Albemarle,* fhall have 40 s. reward, if taken up within the county, 4 l. if elfewhere within the colony, and 10 l. if in any other colony, from
> THOMAS JEFFERSON.

Despite his political stance against slavery, Jefferson owned hundreds of slaves. He posted this ad in search of a runaway slave.

first to ban the import of new enslaved Africans. Jefferson had hoped this would slow the practice of slavery, but the institution continued to grow. Jefferson's draft of an amendment that would free all slaves born after a specific date did not pass.

Jefferson served two one-year terms as governor of Virginia, from 1779 to 1781. After his final term ended, he retired to Monticello, claiming that he would never again enter politics. About political service, he said he had "taken my final leave of everything of that nature, have retired to my farm, my family and books from which I think nothing more will separate me."

Back at home, Jefferson began writing *Notes on the State of Virginia,* in response to questions from a Frenchman about Virginia. Out of political office, he had time to delve into descriptions of the state's history, politics, law, geography, natural resources, economy, social customs, agriculture, and religion.

JEFFERSON ON SLAVERY

Jefferson owned hundreds of enslaved men, women, and children during his lifetime. He relied on their labor to run his plantation at Monticello. Slaves planted and harvested tobacco and other crops, made nails and bricks in Jefferson's workshops, and ran the household—cooking, cleaning, emptying toilets, and caring for Jefferson's children.

Jefferson recognized that slavery opposed the ideals behind the American Revolution. He described slavery as a "moral and political depravity." He worried that it could lead to the downfall of the young nation. Hoping to limit the spread of slavery, in 1784 Jefferson drafted legislation to outlaw slavery in any new federal territories. Congress defeated the bill by one vote.

Jefferson advocated taking steps to abolish slavery over time and to improve the lives of slaves in the meantime. The first step was to end the transatlantic slave trade, preventing traders from importing new slaves into the United States. Second, slave owners needed to lessen the severity of physical punishments and improve living conditions for their slaves. Third, all people born into slavery after a specific date should be freed. Complete abolition, Jefferson believed, would eventually follow. The US government never adopted this plan. Jefferson never believed free black people could integrate into white society. He argued that they were racially inferior, which barred them from ever becoming full citizens of the United States. Instead, he supported colonization—the idea of African Americans resettling in Africa.

Jefferson also used *Notes on the State of Virginia* to address slavery and race. In it he denounced the practice of slavery but claimed that black people were biologically inferior to white people.

A NEW CONSTITUTION

Martha Jefferson died four months after a difficult childbirth, in September 1782. Thomas Jefferson fell into a depression for months, later writing in a letter, "A single event wiped away all my plans and left me a blank which I had not the spirits to fill up."

In the wake of his wife's death, he threw himself back into politics. Later that year, he served as a delegate from Virginia to the Confederation Congress in Philadelphia. The Congress was the governing body of the United States from 1784 to 1789. Jefferson remained in Philadelphia until 1784, when the Congress sent him to Paris, France, with Franklin and Adams to negotiate treaties.

Thomas and Martha Jefferson spent their first winter together in this cabin during the construction of Monticello.

The following year, he learned that the Congress had selected him to be Franklin's replacement as the US minister to France.

Jefferson was in France for five years. During that time, fifty-five delegates from twelve states met at the Constitutional Convention in Philadelphia in 1787 to create a new and permanent federal government. Jefferson and his friend James Madison, a member of the convention, discussed the proceedings in letters. Madison drafted the US Constitution, detailing the form of the new government and broadly outlining its powers.

Jefferson approved of the Constitution overall but complained that it didn't clearly protect personal freedoms

Jefferson (left) served as a US diplomat in France. He exchanged ideas in letters with James Madison (right), who was drafting the US Constitution.

and guard against oppressive government. "What I do not like," he wrote to Madison on December 20, 1787, is "the omission of a bill of rights providing clearly . . . for freedom of religion, freedom of the press, protection against standing armies, restriction against monopolies [protection against illegal arrests], and trials by jury." He added, "I am not a friend to a very [powerful] government. It is always oppressive."

Madison incorporated Jefferson's feedback into a series of proposed changes to the Constitution. Congress approved these changes along with the Constitution in 1789. The required number of states ratified the changes in 1791, and they became the first ten amendments to the Constitution, known together as the Bill of Rights.

Delegates to the convention debated slavery too. Some wanted to abolish the international slave trade, as ten states had already done. But the remaining three states—Georgia, South Carolina, and North Carolina—threatened to leave the convention if the practice was abolished. As a compromise, the convention wrote into the Constitution that the slave trade must remain legal for at least twenty years, until 1808.

SECRETARY OF STATE

Shortly after Jefferson's return from Paris in 1789, the first US president, George Washington, invited him to be the first US secretary of state. Jefferson offered Washington guidance on both international and domestic affairs. He consistently found himself at odds with Alexander Hamilton, the secretary of the treasury. Hamilton advocated governmental policies that strengthened US commerce, cities, and business owners, while Jefferson envisioned the United States as a rural society run by independent farmers.

The first government cabinet, formed by President George Washington, met to discuss various internal and international affairs.

Jefferson and Hamilton's first major conflict centered on the formation of a national central bank. In 1791 Congress passed a plan by Hamilton that created the Bank of the United States. However, the Constitution did not specifically grant such powers to the government. Jefferson believed that the government only had powers the Constitution spelled out for it. He held that the government had to interpret the language of the Constitution strictly. Hamilton, however, advocated for a broader and looser interpretation of the Constitution. He believed that the document's vague language granted the government powers it needed to form a bank. Washington agreed with Hamilton and signed the bill. Tensions between Jefferson and Hamilton grew into a national political rift.

TWO PARTIES

The Federalist Party, the nation's earliest political party, formed around supporters of Alexander Hamilton, who advocated for centralized federal power, a loose interpretation of the Constitution, and a strong financial foundation. Federalists held the presidency from 1789 to 1801, when Thomas Jefferson was elected. They never recovered power, and the party died out by 1817.

The Democratic-Republicans, also called the Jeffersonian Republicans, emerged in the 1790s in response to the Federalists. Led by Thomas Jefferson and James Madison, the Democratic-Republicans held that individual states should have greater power than the federal government and that the government should

strictly adhere to the Constitution as it was written. They thought that a strong central government would lead to abuse of power and was too similar to the British system the United States had overthrown.

Alexander Hamilton's political ideals inspired the Federalist Party's beliefs.

A FRIENDSHIP OF OPPOSITES

In many ways, John Adams and Thomas Jefferson were vastly different both personally and politically. Adams, an outgoing man from Massachusetts, never owned a slave. Jefferson, a quiet man from Virginia, owned hundreds. The short and plump Adams was an exceptional speaker. Tall, slim Jefferson was notorious for his poor public speaking. Federalist Adams believed in a strong central government, while Democratic-Republican Jefferson thought power should reside with the states. Yet the two had become close friends during the Continental Congress in 1775, when Adams helped Jefferson write the Declaration of Independence.

Relations between Jefferson and Adams cooled, however, as partisan politics divided the nation. In the late 1790s, during Adams's presidency, their opposing political stances led to a deep rift. Their friendship eventually revived after Jefferson's retirement from the presidency.

The clashes between Jefferson and Hamilton continued despite pleas from Washington to make peace. Jefferson increasingly felt that he was losing influence with the president. In 1793, during Washington's second term, Jefferson resigned as secretary of state and retired once more to Monticello.

Jefferson remained at Monticello until 1796, when a group of prominent Democratic-Republicans in Congress selected him as their presidential candidate. Washington's vice president, John Adams, narrowly defeated Jefferson in the election. Jefferson, the candidate with the second-highest number of votes, became

vice president, as was the practice at the time. As a Democratic-Republican in a Federalist-controlled government, Jefferson was given very little to do. He found the position "honorable and easy," and spent much of his time presiding over the Senate. He also wrote *A Manual of Parliamentary Practice,* a book that provided guidelines for Senate procedures.

★ CHAPTER TWO ★

PRESIDENT JEFFERSON'S FIRST TERM

John Adams and Thomas Jefferson, once close friends, found themselves pitted against each other in the presidential election of 1800. This election was a battle of Adams's Federalists against Jefferson's Democratic-Republicans.

Bitter personal insults and accusations flew back and forth during the presidential campaign. Federalists claimed Jefferson was a "howling atheist" because of his support of the freedom to practice any religion—or none. They also called him a coward for not fighting in the revolution. Democratic-Republicans, meanwhile, decried Adams as a monarchist who wanted to be more like a king than a

John Adams ran against Jefferson in the 1800 presidential election.

Federalists harshly criticized Jefferson during the election of 1800. This political cartoon, drawn during the election, depicts Jefferson trying to destroy the Constitution.

president. Adams did favor an authoritarian president, believing it was necessary to protect the country from falling into chaos and disunity.

During this period, presidential candidates did not have vice presidential running mates. Instead, each party nominated two candidates for president—a first choice and a second. Members of the Electoral College each cast two votes for president. The candidate with the most votes was elected president, while the second-place candidate became vice president.

THE TWELFTH AMENDMENT

In response to the messy election of 1800, Congress passed the Twelfth Amendment in 1804 to prevent such a situation from happening again. Instead of the members of the Electoral College casting two votes each for president, this amendment requires separate votes for the presidential and vice presidential candidates.

In the election of 1800, Charles Pinckney, the Federalists' second-choice candidate, earned sixty-four electoral votes. John Adams secured sixty-five votes. Jefferson and fellow Democratic-Republican Aaron Burr, the party's second choice for president, each received seventy-three. The Constitution declared that in the case of a tie, the House of Representatives would make the decision. On February 17, after thirty-six rounds of voting, the deadlock ended and Thomas Jefferson was declared the third president of the United States, with Burr as vice president.

FEDERALISTS VS. DEMOCRATIC-REPUBLICANS

In his inaugural address, Thomas Jefferson aimed to heal the divide between Federalists and Democratic-Republicans. "Every difference of opinion is not a difference of principle," he stated. He reminded the parties that they were all working toward the same goal—the success of the nation.

Presidents Washington and Adams had been Federalists, and after Democratic-Republicans won a majority of seats in Congress as well as the presidency, Jefferson called the victories the Revolution of 1800. It was the first time voters had

elected a president from a different political party, setting the stage for an enduring two-party system. In a letter, Jefferson explained, "[T]he revolution of 1800, for that was as real a revolution in the principles of our government as that of 1776 was in its form; not effected indeed by the sword, as that, but by the rational and peaceable instrument of reform, the suffrage of the people."

The people, Jefferson believed, were unhappy with his predecessors' strong governing style, which he viewed as being like that of royalty. By electing Democratic-Republicans, Americans were voting for a more democratic government that would respond to the will of the people.

Jefferson distanced himself from the previous administrations in ways large and small. Washington and Adams, for instance, had both delivered their annual State of the Union addresses to Congress in person. Jefferson thought this was too similar to how the British king addressed Parliament. Because of this—and also, likely, because of his intense dislike of public speaking—Jefferson sent a written message to Congress each year, to be read there by a clerk. This practice continued until President Woodrow Wilson delivered his message in person in 1913.

Jefferson also worked to create an air of informality at the President's House, as the White House was called until around 1811. When Augustus J. Foster, a British diplomat, visited Jefferson, he was shocked to discover the president "dressed [down] and look[ing] extremely like a very plain farmer, and wear[ing] his slippers down at his heels." Jefferson also ended the practice of seating dinner guests based on their status, with people of higher status placed closer to the president. Instead, he allowed guests to choose their own seats, a style called pell-mell.

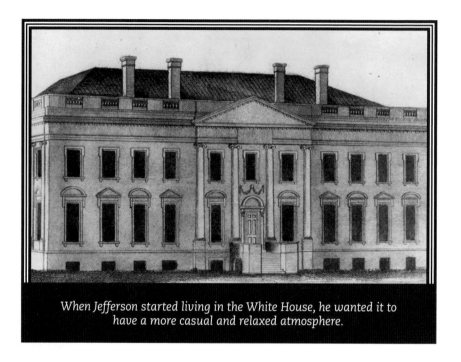

When Jefferson started living in the White House, he wanted it to have a more casual and relaxed atmosphere.

A REVOLUTIONARY FISCAL POLICY

Upon taking office, Jefferson chose a cabinet of like-minded experts. Among his advisers were future president James Madison as secretary of state, Henry Dearborn as secretary of war, Robert Smith as secretary of the navy, and Levi Lincoln as attorney general. Jefferson also named Albert Gallatin, a Swiss-born veteran of the American Revolution, as secretary of the treasury.

One of the highest priorities of Jefferson's early administration was eliminating the national debt and decreasing citizens' taxes. Both Gallatin and Jefferson recognized that borrowing money and collecting taxes were necessary to pay for the nation's expenses. However, they also wanted to use tax money from citizens to spur the country's growth by funneling that money back into businesses and farms.

DOLLEY MADISON, THE PRESIDENTRESS

Thomas Jefferson never remarried after his wife, Martha, died in 1782. As president, when he needed a cohost at White House events, he often asked Dolley Madison, the wife of his secretary of state, James. Fashionable and socially skilled, Madison took a more active and public role than had the first two presidents' wives, Martha Washington and Abigail Adams. She engaged with visiting politicians and members of the general public and also raised money and support for the Lewis and Clark expedition. At the time, there was no name for the president's spouse or cohost. Madison's popularity and service earned her the nickname the Presidentress. When her husband was elected president after Jefferson, she

served as his cohost and political partner from 1809 to 1817. At Dolley Madison's funeral in 1849, then president Zachary Taylor praised her, using the term First Lady for the first time.

Dolley Madison cohosted many White House and political events with Jefferson.

Jefferson entrusted Gallatin with creating a plan for reducing and eventually paying off the debt. The United States had borrowed large sums of money from other countries during the American Revolution, and the Washington and Adams administrations had later added $10 million to the national debt. By the time Jefferson took office, the country had a deficit of $83 million. Nevertheless, Gallatin created a plan to completely eliminate the national debt over the course of about seventeen years.

Albert Gallatin was Jefferson's secretary of the treasury.

Gallatin's plan trimmed the nation's spending while also cutting taxes. Much of the annual budget, approximately $3 million, was spent on the standing army. Gallatin reduced this military spending by half, downsizing the army to just three thousand soldiers and cutting the navy to just thirteen ships. Gallatin's plan also repealed internal taxes on goods and property. These taxes included the unpopular whiskey excise tax, an extra charge on all alcoholic spirits produced in the United States. This one tax made up the majority of the $600,000 that the government received from taxes each year, but it was also among the few taxes that individuals paid directly. Farmers who made whiskey from their extra grain had resisted paying this tax for

years. George Washington had even sent troops to quell a violent protest in western Pennsylvania in 1794 that became known as the Whiskey Rebellion.

Gallatin and Jefferson both wanted to avoid taxing citizens directly. Instead of these internal taxes, the government relied on import taxes, which businesses paid on goods brought into the country. These taxes could run as high as 50 percent of a product's price.

At the end of his first year as secretary of the treasury, Albert Gallatin had eliminated $2 million of the nation's debt. By the time President Jefferson left office in 1809, the debt had decreased by $26 million. The Democratic-Republican government maintained the plan Gallatin had put in place and paid off the last of the debt in January 1833.

Some US citizens protested the whiskey tax by tarring and feathering tax collectors and burning their homes. Jefferson and Gallatin lifted this tax.

FIFTH *CONGRESS* OF THE UNITED STATES:

At the Second Session.

Begun and held at the city of *Philadelphia*, in the state of PENNSYLVANIA, on *Monday*, the thirteenth of *November*, one thousand seven hundred and ninety-seven.

An ACT *concerning aliens.*

BE it enacted by the Senate and House of Representatives of the United States of America, in Congress assembled, *That it is*

The Alien and Sedition Acts allowed the president to deport any noncitizen he claimed to be dangerous.

THE ALIEN AND SEDITION ACTS

Early in his presidency, Jefferson confronted another legacy from his predecessor: the Alien and Sedition Acts. Passed by the Federalist Congress in 1798, during Adams's presidency, this series of four laws—the Naturalization, Alien Friends, Alien Enemies, and Sedition Acts—had drawn immense public criticism. The laws authorized the president to deport noncitizens considered to be dangerous, even if the nation was not at war, and at times of war to detain and deport any male noncitizens from an enemy nation. The acts also greatly increased the amount of time an immigrant needed to live in the United States before becoming a naturalized citizen, and they legalized the imprisonment of anyone who produced "any false, scandalous and malicious writing" about the government or elected officials.

Jefferson, who had been vice president at the time, saw these laws not only as violations of the Bill of Rights but also as clear attempts to weaken the Democratic-Republican Party. The first three acts specifically targeted immigrants in the United States, who often supported the Democratic-Republican Party. These potential Democratic-Republican voters would have to wait an additional nine years before gaining citizenship. Throughout that time, they were at risk of imprisonment and deportation. Furthermore, the Sedition Act prevented people in the United States from speaking ill of elected government officials. This law specifically targeted people who disagreed with the Federalists. Finally, the text of the law exempted only "the government of the United States, or either house of the Congress of the United States, or the President of the United States." The vice president (Jefferson) was absent from the law's protection.

Jefferson was not the only person to oppose the Alien and Sedition Acts. The widespread unpopularity of the acts prompted many Federalist supporters to change loyalties in the 1800 election. This helped to elect not only Jefferson but also many other Democratic-Republicans.

The Alien Friends Act had expired in 1800 without deporting any noncitizens. In 1802 Jefferson's administration repealed the 1798 Naturalization Act, returning the required period of residency for citizenship to five years. The Alien Enemies Act, however, stood for more than a century.

By the time the Sedition Act expired on March 3, 1801—the day before Jefferson took the oath of office—twenty-five people had been arrested under it. Early in his presidency, Jefferson pardoned the men convicted under the act and vowed to repay their fines. Among the pardoned was James Callender, a newspaper reporter with the reputation of spreading scandal. During Adams's presidency, Jefferson had paid Callender to write

articles criticizing the Federalists. Callender had been jailed and fined $200 for criticizing President Adams in print. After being pardoned, Callender demanded that Jefferson repay his fine and give him a government job. If not, Callender said, he would reveal damaging personal information about the president. When he received his money but not a job, Callender felt betrayed, and he made good on his threat. In September 1802, the *Richmond Recorder* of Virginia published Callender's article claiming the president had fathered children with one of his slaves, Sally Hemings, a daughter of Elizabeth Hemings. The antislavery Federalist Party spread the rumor to discredit the president and the institution of slavery.

THE MIDNIGHT JUDGES

Upon entering the presidency, Jefferson inherited last-minute changes in the federal court system. During his final months in office, marked by the presidential-election tie between Jefferson and Burr, President Adams did not know whom the House would choose to take his place. He knew only that the new president would be a Democratic-Republican. With the nation's future leadership uncertain, the president signed the Judiciary Act of 1801 on February 13. This law decreased the number of Supreme Court justices from six to five and created new judgeships for lower-level courts. President Adams quickly appointed Federalist judges to these new positions before leaving office. The last-minute nature of these appointments earned them the nickname the midnight judges.

The Supreme Court had long desired these reforms, but the Democratic-Republicans saw the measures as Federalists' attempts to increase their own influence and to weaken the power of state courts. Jefferson and his cabinet were set on repealing the act, and a year later, they passed the Judiciary Act of 1802. This new law eliminated the courts the Federalists had created.

JEFFERSON AND HEMINGS

Jefferson said it was beneath him to respond publicly to the rumor of his sexual liaison with his slave Sally Hemings. As a teenager, Hemings had served as a maid to Jefferson's youngest daughter, Mary, while the Jeffersons lived in Paris, France. Afterward, Hemings was a house servant at Monticello. When her son Madison Hemings told his life story to a reporter in 1873, he said his father, Thomas Jefferson, had promised Sally Hemings that he would free their children, and in fact, her family members were the only slaves Jefferson freed in his will.

Evidence is strong that Jefferson and Hemings did have children together. DNA tests in 1998 proved that Hemings's descendants have a male Jefferson ancestor, and while the test cannot pinpoint Thomas, the timing of his visits to Monticello match up with the birthdates of Sally Hemings's children.

Descendants of Sally Hemings pose at a family reunion at Monticello in 2003. According to family members who have researched the subject, they are among the descendants of Hemings and Thomas Jefferson.

MARBURY V. MADISON

The political fallout of Adams's appointments did not end there. Outgoing Secretary of State John Marshall had not sent out all of Adams's official last-minute appointments for the new judgeships. When Madison became Jefferson's secretary of state in March 1801, he discovered a stack of these commissions on his desk. Together, he and Jefferson decided against sending them out.

One of the undelivered commissions was meant for a man named William Marbury, whom President Adams had named as a justice of the peace in Washington, DC. When Marbury did not receive his appointment, he pressed charges against Madison and took his case directly to the Supreme Court. Marbury pushed for the court to issue a writ of mandamus—a court order that would have legally forced Madison to deliver the appointment to Marbury.

William Marbury was supposed to receive an appointment as a justice of the peace.

Chief Justice John Marshall, Adams's former secretary of state—the very official who had neglected to send out Marbury's appointment—delivered the court's opinion on *Marbury v. Madison* on February 24, 1803. He declared that Marbury had a right to receive his appointment—and lectured Jefferson's

administration on the importance of government officials fulfilling their duties. However, Marshall then stated that the Supreme Court did not have the right to issue the writ Marbury had demanded. He argued that the law that made this writ possible, the Judiciary Act of 1789, was actually unconstitutional. Marshall was saying that even presidents

Chief Justice John Marshall oversaw the Marbury v. Madison *case.*

should honor their commitments without being forced to do so by writ.

Marshall's decision introduced the concept of judicial review and established the court's role of interpreting the Constitution. He claimed that if a law conflicts with the Constitution, it is up to the court to "determine which of the conflicting rules governs the case." In writing his decision, Marshall elevated the Supreme Court and made it possible for the court to strike down laws and statutes that it deemed unconstitutional.

WAR ON THE JUDICIARY

In late 1803, in the wake of the *Marbury v. Madison* ruling, the Jefferson administration started trying to remove Federalists

from their posts in the Federalist-controlled federal courts. They targeted these judges in retaliation for their actions against Democratic-Republicans under the Sedition Act and planned to replace them with Jefferson supporters. Judgeships, however, were granted for life. For Jefferson to replace these judges, he needed to successfully impeach them—have them tried and found guilty of misconduct.

The Democratic-Republicans managed to impeach Judge John Pickering from New Hampshire. An aging alcoholic, Pickering had exhibited bizarre behavior on the bench. Still, according to the Constitution, federal officials could only be impeached from their posts for "treason, bribery, or other high crimes and misdemeanors." Pickering had committed no crime against the state. However, Congress did impeach and remove the judge.

John Pickering was impeached from his position as a New Hampshire judge.

Jefferson's administration then turned its attention to Associate Supreme Court Justice Samuel Chase. Chase had been responsible for convicting James Callender under the Sedition Act. He had also criticized the repeal of the Judiciary Act of 1801, which the House of

Representatives used as grounds to impeach the judge. During his trial in 1805, however, the Senate did not convict him of any wrongdoing. This failure to remove Chase marked the end of the Jefferson administration's attempts to remove Federalist judges from the courts.

★ CHAPTER THREE ★

THE BARBARY WAR AND THE LOUISIANA PURCHASE

Within three months of Jefferson's 1801 inauguration, the United States was at war, the result of a conflict that had been brewing for two hundred years. Since the seventeenth century, corsairs, or pirates, from independent states on the Barbary Coast of North Africa had practiced state-sponsored piracy. These corsairs captured merchant ships in the Mediterranean Sea and held their crews and cargoes hostage for ransom. The ransom then went to the corsairs' sponsoring state, increasing the wealth and naval power of those nations.

Over the years, Great Britain and France had decided it was better to pay annual tributes to the Barbary states than to pay ransom for each captured vessel. These tributes allowed ships from these nations and their colonies to sail freely through the Mediterranean.

After gaining independence, the United States was no longer protected by Great Britain's tributes. As Washington's secretary of state, Jefferson had opposed the United States agreeing to pay its own tribute. Only a show of force against the Barbary states would resolve the issue, he thought. To James Monroe, he argued,

Barbary corsairs patrolled the Mediterranean Sea off the coast of North Africa and held ships hostage if they hadn't paid an annual tribute.

"The states must see the rod; perhaps it must be felt by some one of them." Jefferson also wanted to build up the small US Navy to battle the corsairs.

President Washington and Vice President Adams disagreed with Jefferson. In 1795 Washington's administration signed peace treaties with the Barbary states of Algiers (in modern Algeria), Tunis (in modern Tunisia), and Tripoli (in modern Libya), agreeing to pay tribute for the safe passage of its merchant ships. The United States also paid nearly $1 million to retrieve eighty-three US sailors Algiers had held since 1784.

WAR

As Jefferson had predicted, the corsairs continued to demand more money from the United States. When Jefferson took office in 1801, Yusuf Karamanli, the pasha, or ruler, of Tripoli demanded a new treaty. Karamanli wanted the United States to pay Tripoli $250,000 immediately, as well as an annual sum of $50,000.

FIRE AND SAND

Two actions in the Barbary War showed sacrifice and courage on the part of the US forces. In 1803 Tripoli captured a US warship, the *Philadelphia,* and held hostage the 307 crew members. In February 1804, Lieutenant Stephen Decatur led a small group of Marines in a nighttime attack in Tripoli Harbor. They set fire to the *Philadelphia,* destroying their own ship rather than letting the pirates have it. According to legend, British naval hero Horatio Nelson lauded the sacrifice as "the most bold and daring act of the age."

The next year, US Marine Corps lieutenant Presley O'Bannon led a small force of Marines and several hundred paid mercenaries in a 500-mile (805-km) march across the desert,

from Egypt to Tripoli. There they captured the port city of Derne. This battle, the first US land battle on foreign soil, was memorialized in the opening lines of the "Marines' Hymn" by an unknown author: "From the Halls of Montezuma, to the shores of Tripoli."

US Marines set fire to the Philadelphia, their own ship, because they didn't want the Tripoli pirates to keep it.

Jefferson told Madison, "I know that nothing will stop the eternal increase from these pirates but the presence of an armed force." Jefferson denied the pasha's requests and ordered Commodore Richard Dale to set sail for the Mediterranean with four ships. If he learned that Tripoli had declared war on the United States, Dale and his men were instructed to "chastise [Tripoli's] insolence . . . by sinking, burning, or destroying their ships and vessels wherever you shall find them." Jefferson also wanted Dale's force to blockade Barbary harbors. Upon arriving at the Mediterranean, Dale received word that Karamanli had declared war on the United States on May 14, before Dale had even sailed.

After four years of hostilities, in 1805 US troops launched a two-pronged attack on Tripoli. While US Marines marched overland to Tripoli, the US Navy blockaded Tripoli Harbor. Under pressure, Karamanli accepted defeat and signed a peace treaty on June 5, 1805. The treaty stipulated that the United States would no longer pay tribute to Tripoli. Congress ratified the treaty, and Jefferson signed it on April 12, 1806.

Commodore Richard Dale led an attack against the Barbary pirates.

In addition to attacking Tripoli on land, the US Navy blockaded the Tripoli Harbor with gunboats.

Jefferson's aggressive stance in the First Barbary War (1801–1805) showed the world that the young nation was a force to be reckoned with. However, victory provided the United States with only limited safety in the Mediterranean. Other Barbary states, such as Algeria, still demanded money from the United States. It was not until the United States defeated Algeria in the Second Barbary War (1815), after Jefferson's presidency, that the nation was finally free from paying tribute to Mediterranean pirates.

CRAMPED FOR SPACE

At the time the First Barbary War started, the United States stretched from the Atlantic Ocean in the east to the Mississippi River in the west, and from British-held Canada in the north to Spanish-held Florida in the south. Most Americans lived no more than 50 miles (80 km) from the Atlantic Ocean. However, more and more Americans were moving away from the crowded eastern coast. As they migrated west of the Appalachian Mountains toward the Mississippi River, the waterway became a major route for US trade and transportation. Tobacco, bacon,

butter, whiskey, salt, potatoes, and other goods traveled down the river to the Gulf of Mexico. At the end of the journey was New Orleans, a thriving port city at the mouth of the Mississippi—and outside of the United States. Access to this city was crucial to US trade.

In 1795 the United States and Spain had signed the Pinckney Treaty, which allowed US merchants to use the Mississippi River without paying a tax. The treaty also gave the United States the right of deposit, or permission to temporarily store goods along the river before loading them onto oceangoing merchant ships.

Still, Jefferson wanted greater access to the West than this agreement with Spain provided. France, a powerful empire ruled by the ambitious Napoleon Bonaparte, claimed the land west of the Mississippi, known as the Louisiana Territory.

The Mississippi was a crucial route for moving people and goods, such as the cargo being transported on this flatboat.

Jefferson did not believe that the United States and France could peacefully share North America. He saw France's possession of the territory as "the embryo of a tornado which will burst on the countries on both sides of the Atlantic and involve in its effects their highest destinies."

In 1802 Spain revoked the United States' right of deposit in New Orleans and gave control of the city to France. Outraged Federalists called for the United States to seize the port city.

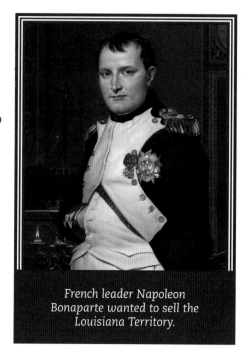

French leader Napoleon Bonaparte wanted to sell the Louisiana Territory.

Jefferson ignored them. He predicted that trying to take the city by force would result in "seven years [of] war, the loss of one hundred thousand lives . . . and that demoralization which war superinduces on the human mind." Instead of pursuing military action, Jefferson wanted to approach France with an offer to buy New Orleans.

THE LOUISIANA PURCHASE AGREEMENT

Jefferson authorized the US minister to France, Robert Livingston, to offer the French $10 million in exchange for New Orleans and Florida (which Jefferson incorrectly believed Spain had also ceded to France) or, if that failed, to buy access to the city's port. Jefferson sent his friend and ally James Monroe to help Livingston with the negotiations. Upon arrival in Paris in April 1803, Monroe learned that the evening before, France's foreign minister, Charles Maurice de Talleyrand, had offered Livingston not only New Orleans but the entire Louisiana Territory. "The field open to us is infinitely larger than our instructions contemplated," Livingston wrote to Madison.

Previously, Napoleon had wanted to increase France's empire with North American landholdings. His troops, however, were losing the fight to put down a slave rebellion in the French colony of Saint-Domingue. This conflict, the Haitian Revolution (1791–1804), would end in November when the victorious revolutionaries established the Republic of Haiti. Meanwhile, Napoleon realized that possession of these distant territories was straining the nation's finances. Napoleon did not want this cost, particularly as he was set on conquering Europe. France's finance minister advised Napoleon to unload the unwanted land by selling the entire Louisiana Territory to the United States.

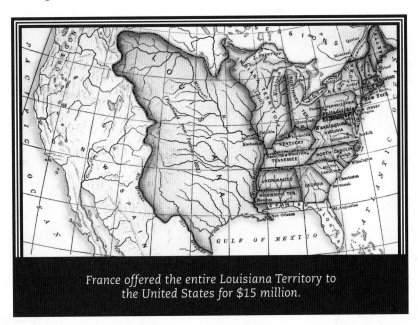

France offered the entire Louisiana Territory to the United States for $15 million.

THE HAITIAN REVOLUTION

The Haitian Revolution in the French Caribbean slave colony of Saint-Domingue was the world's largest successful revolt of enslaved people. The revolutionaries were inspired partly by the Declaration of the Rights of Man, a document the French legislature had passed in 1789. Thomas Jefferson himself had inspired this declaration of human rights, which was similar to his draft of the US Declaration of Independence. But although Jefferson supported the ideal of universal freedom, he feared the Haitians' overthrow of white domination would inspire US slaves to rebel too. He wrote to James Monroe in 1793, "It is high time we should foresee the bloody scenes which our

Encouraged by the French Declaration of the Rights of Man, slaves rebelled in the French colony of Saint-Domingue.

children, and possibly ourselves . . . [will] have to wade through, and try to avert them." Indeed, the revolution did help inspire many African Americans in the United States in their long struggle against slavery.

Jefferson worked to quell the Haitian Revolution. As secretary of state, he authorized sending one thousand guns and $40,000 to aid French slave owners. When he became president, Jefferson discontinued antislavery president John Adams's policy of US aid to Haitian revolutionary leader Toussaint L'Ouverture.

In 1803 the Haitians, led by former slave Jean-Jacques Dessalines, defeated Napoleon's army and massacred most of the remaining white population. The Republic of Haiti was the second country in the Americas to gain independence. The first country to do so, the United States, did not recognize Haiti's independence until 1862.

Toussaint L'Ouverture led the Haitian Revolution until he was arrested in 1802. He died in a French prison in 1803.

Livingston and Monroe recognized the value of the deal and quickly began negotiations with Talleyrand. By April 30, they had come to an agreement. The United States would purchase the Louisiana Territory for $15 million. Monroe and Livingston had bought approximately 828,000 square miles (2,144,510 sq. km) of land at about 3 cents per acre (0.4 hectare). The purchase nearly doubled the size of their young nation for only $5 million more than the amount Jefferson had authorized for the purchase of a single city.

James Monroe helped negotiate the Louisiana Purchase.

Word of the treaty reached Thomas Jefferson on the evening of July 3, 1803, and the president announced the historic agreement on the Fourth of July. "The future inhabitants of the Atlantic and Mississippi states will be our sons," he wrote. Many Americans met the news of the acquisition with excitement. "Every face wears a smile, and every heart leaps with Joy," future president Andrew Jackson wrote to Jefferson. However, others criticized the expense, complaining that the country already had more land than money. Indeed, Jefferson's administration had to borrow money from abroad to meet the purchase price.

CONSTITUTIONAL CONCERNS

Jefferson was pleased with the agreement. However, he and his secretary of state, James Madison, had concerns about the constitutionality of such a purchase. "The [C]onstitution has made no provision for our holding foreign territory, still less for incorporating foreign nations into our Union," Jefferson wrote in a letter in August 1803. He believed Congress would need to amend the Constitution to allow the government to buy and govern the territory. He even drafted a version of the amendment.

However, a letter from Livingston and Monroe revealed that Napoleon felt mounting anxiety about the agreement, and the US government only had until October 30 to approve the treaty. With this news, Jefferson had Congress move forward with ratification. He concluded that nobody would question the agreement's constitutionality because of its unmistakable value to the United States.

On October 20, the Senate voted 24–7 to approve the treaty. In December 1803, the United States formally assumed control over the territory. Europeans had never mapped this land, so the boundaries of the territory were not clearly set. Ultimately, it was determined that the United States owned the land from the Mississippi River west to the Rocky Mountains, between Canada in the north and the Gulf of Mexico in the south. It took until well into the nineteenth century for the northern and southern borders to be established with Great Britain and Spain. Florida was not included in the purchase. The United States would acquire West Florida in 1810 and East Florida in 1821 from Spain.

★ CHAPTER FOUR ★

THE CORPS OF DISCOVERY AND AMERICAN INDIANS

Even before France's unexpected offer, the president intended to explore the land west of the Mississippi River. In January 1803, Jefferson wrote to Congress detailing his plans for exploration of the West. He asked Congress for $2,500 to fund a transcontinental journey of "an intelligent officer, with ten or twelve chosen men, fit for enterprise [to explore] to the Western Ocean." He wanted the men to locate the Northwest Passage, a legendary waterway mistakenly thought to connect the Missouri River to the Pacific Ocean. Travel on such a water route would be immensely easier than overland trips. Jefferson was also curious about the area's American Indian populations, its plant and animal life, and its other natural features.

To Congress, Jefferson framed his anticipated expeditionary force—the Corps of Volunteers for North Western Discovery, or the Corps of Discovery—as explorers motivated by scientific

discovery and commerce. The corps would document their observations of the environment and develop trade relations with American Indians on the way to the Pacific. The group would also solidify the nation's claim to these distant lands, warning European powers to stay out of US territories and making the West more accessible to US settlers.

JEFFERSON'S AMERICAN INDIAN POLICY

Jefferson's message to Congress also described his American Indian policy. He wanted to develop good trade relations with native nations. He also wanted them to abandon what he considered a savage lifestyle based on hunting, which requires huge amounts of land, in favor of farming, which requires less. Jefferson promoted what he saw as a civilized farming lifestyle that would settle American Indians in one place and also encourage them to sell their land to the United States.

The Missouri River (above) was mistakenly believed to be connected to the Pacific Ocean by a waterway called the Northwest Passage.

JEFFERSON'S FRONTIER

Jefferson felt the allure of the frontier all his life. Shadwell, Jefferson's childhood home, was in the foothills of the Blue Ridge Mountains in western Virginia—on the western frontier of the thirteen colonies. Peter Jefferson had been among the first settlers in the region, and as a surveyor, in 1751 he created the first accurate map of Virginia. He was also a member of the Loyal Company, which arranged an expedition to explore the Missouri River and discover whether it flowed west to the Pacific Ocean. The exploration, however, was canceled before it began.

Prior to founding the Corps of Discovery, Jefferson had twice attempted to send explorers to the western frontier. He tried to recruit surveyor George Rogers Clark (the brother of future Corps of Discovery leader William Clark) for an expedition in 1783 and made a similar offer to French botanist André Michaux in 1793. Neither mission came to pass.

He wrote, "In leading them to agriculture, to manufactures, and civilization; in bringing together their and our settlements, and in preparing them ultimately to participate in the benefits of our governments, I trust and believe we are acting for their greatest good."

The president hoped to ensure peace on the frontier and to guarantee that American Indian nations would be allies if the United States fell into conflict with European powers on the continent—such as Spain in Florida or Great Britain in Canada.

Jefferson insisted that his agents must not pressure American

Indian nations to sell their lands. He did, however, suggest that US agents sell goods to the nations on credit. He hoped that if American Indians were unable to pay their debts, they would offer up their lands as payment. The US government would then use those lands to encourage white settlement.

Congress approved Jefferson's requests for funds on February 28, 1803. Jefferson selected his personal secretary and distant cousin, Meriwether Lewis, to lead the expedition. Lewis was a captain in the US Army and had knowledge of the West. Lewis chose William Clark, his former military commander, as his coleader. Four years older than twenty-eight-year-old Lewis, Clark was a skilled mapmaker, riverman, and leader.

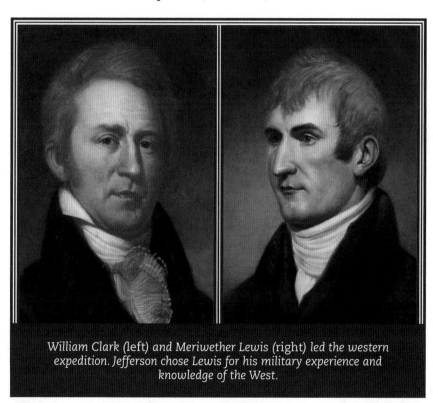

William Clark (left) and Meriwether Lewis (right) led the western expedition. Jefferson chose Lewis for his military experience and knowledge of the West.

JEFFERSON'S INSTRUCTIONS

Jefferson wrote detailed instructions to Lewis on June 20, 1803. Lewis's most important task, Jefferson said, was to find the Northwest Passage to the ocean. Jefferson, with his wide-ranging interests, also instructed Lewis to map the interior of North America; to note plants and their characteristics; to record weather patterns; to determine the potential for trading and fur trapping in the West; and to send back copies of the expedition's journals, notes, and observations at regular intervals. Jefferson also asked the corps to document animal life, including the presence of mammoths. Jefferson, with his interest in science, had obtained bones of these giant, elephant-like mammals (actually American mastodons) and hoped to hear news of live ones. In fact, the mammoth was extinct.

Jefferson informed Lewis that he was to treat the indigenous peoples he met along the way "in the most friendly & conciliatory manner." Jefferson knew that gift exchanges demonstrated friendship and goodwill, so he directed Lewis to bring presents for American Indian groups. Jefferson reminded the expedition to establish trade relations with indigenous nations. He also instructed Lewis and his men to record native languages, cultural practices, foods, physical characteristics, and the extent of their lands.

THE EXPEDITION

On May 14, 1804, Lewis and Clark and nearly fifty men, including Clark's slave, York, departed from Saint Louis, Missouri. Lewis and Clark later hired a young woman named Sacagawea, of the Shoshone Nation, and her husband, French Canadian trader Toussaint Charbonneau, to serve as interpreters in encounters with American Indian groups.

SACAGAWEA

The most famed relationship the corps developed was with their Shoshone translator, Sacagawea. Clark recorded the pronunciation of her name as "Sah-cah' gah-we-ah." As a child, she had been captured by the Hidatsa Nation. Toussaint Charbonneau later made her one of his two wives. About sixteen years old when she joined the corps, Sacagawea traveled with the explorers from present-day North Dakota to the Pacific Ocean and back—carrying her baby son for much of the journey. Her language skills were invaluable to the expedition, as was her knowledge of the terrain and her ability to identify edible roots, berries, and other plants. Thomas Jefferson's administration offered her no compensation or recognition for her service with the Corps of Discovery, although her husband received $500.33 and 320 acres (129 hectares) of land. Sacagawea reportedly died in 1812, at the age of about twenty-four.

Sacagawea shows Lewis and Clark Three Forks, Montana. Clark's slave, York (second from left), accompanied them on the expedition.

The expedition met people from nearly fifty American Indian nations, including the Mandan, Nez Percé, Cheyenne, Chinook, Pawnee, and Crow. A meeting with Blackfeet Indians in Montana ended in bloodshed after the explorers killed two Blackfeet warriors trying to steal the expedition's guns. In northwestern Oregon, where the corps built a winter home, Fort Clatsop, the expedition became trading partners with Coboway, a Clatsop chief.

Upon first meeting a new group of American Indians, the explorers would inform them that their land was now part of the United States and that they had a new "Great Father" in Washington, DC: President Thomas Jefferson. Lewis and Clark encouraged the nations' leaders to travel to Washington to meet Jefferson. (Members of the Choctaw, Cherokee, and other nations eventually did so.) Then the expedition members offered peace medals and other gifts, such as tobacco, mirrors, ivory combs, and colored glass beads. From Lewis and Clark's perspective, acceptance of the peace medal meant acceptance of Jefferson as the Great Father. The American Indians, however, saw the medals only as part of the customary trading of gifts between equals.

In April a group of about twelve explorers headed back down the Missouri River with the expedition's first findings. In August a delighted Jefferson received the shipments: maps and copious notes; plant specimens and seeds; two kinds of live birds (magpie and grouse); a live prairie dog; elk horns; mineral and soil samples; animal skins and skeletons; and various items made by American Indians, including buffalo robes, bows and arrows, and clay pots.

Finding the Northwest Passage remained the corps's main priority. In August 1805, following a winding trail through the Rocky Mountains, the expedition members discovered the

Lewis and Clark collected and preserved many plant specimens on their expedition.

Missouri River's source. They climbed a ridge above it, expecting to see the Pacific Ocean beyond, but only saw more mountains. The explorers realized that there was no water route to the Pacific. The dream of the Northwest Passage was dead.

The expedition forged ahead. After traveling nearly another 500 miles (805 km), they finally spotted the bay leading to the Pacific Ocean on November 7, 1805. William Clark, with his usual poor spelling, recorded the moment in his journal: "Ocian in view! O! the joy . . ."

After waiting out the winter, the Corps of Discovery turned toward home in March 1806. The members of the expedition received a hero's welcome when they arrived in Saint Louis on September 23, 1806. Jefferson had estimated that the journey would last a year, but it had taken two years and four months.

Many people back east had assumed the corps had not survived. The group had journeyed more than 8,000 miles (12,874 km), losing just one member during the treacherous trip. (He had died from a burst appendix.)

The expedition revealed the West to be far more expansive and geographically diverse than Jefferson had expected. Members' journals recorded wonders of the West, including grizzly bears and herds of thousands of buffalo (American bison). They showed that the vast Louisiana Territory was rich in mineral resources, precious metals, fertile soil, forests, grazing land, and wildlife. As the nation grew,

The findings of Lewis and Clark's expedition inspired colonists to migrate westward, onto American Indian lands.

President Jefferson encouraged westward migration onto American Indian lands. Over the course of his presidency, his administration bought almost 200,000 square miles (517,998 sq. km) of land from American Indian nations. Jefferson's successors would continue to expand on his policies of purchasing native lands and encouraging US settlement in the West, often with devastating consequences for American Indian nations.

CHAPTER FIVE

JEFFERSON'S SECOND TERM

In the 1804 presidential election, Jefferson had handily defeated his Federalist challenger, Charles Pinckney, who received just 14 electoral votes to Jefferson's 162. Jefferson's second term had begun on a high note, and he seemed poised to build on these successes. In his 1806 annual message to Congress, Jefferson reported with satisfaction that the conflict in Tripoli "had been amicably and justly terminated" and that the Corps of Discovery had returned from its trip to the Pacific Ocean with "all the success which could have been expected." However, the remainder of Jefferson's second term was fraught with challenges and frustrations.

US artist Rembrandt Peale painted this portrait of Jefferson in 1805.

AARON BURR

Jefferson and his old political rival, Alexander Hamilton, had continued to differ on almost every point except one—that Jefferson's first vice president, Aaron Burr, was not fit for political office. In his reelection campaign, President Jefferson had replaced Burr with George Clinton as his running mate. Burr, meanwhile, heard that Hamilton had insulted his character, and he wrote a letter challenging Hamilton to a duel. The European ritual of dueling as a way for elite men to avenge their wounded pride had become popular among US politicians. Rather than apologizing, which would have ended the contest, Hamilton wrote back defiantly. On July 11, 1804, the men faced each other over pistols. Hamilton shot and missed, possibly on purpose. Burr shot Hamilton in the abdomen, a wound from which Hamilton died the next day. Burr was charged with murder but never faced trial. Jefferson never commented publicly on the death of his rival.

Aaron Burr challenged Alexander Hamilton to a duel after Hamilton insulted him.

Burr finished his term as vice president, but he had ruined his political reputation. He traveled west to the lower Mississippi River valley, from whence rumors about his plotting began to reach President Jefferson. Some reports suggested that Burr was preparing to wage war with Mexico, lay claim to the southwestern United States for himself, and carve out his own territory to rule.

Aaron Burr served as Jefferson's first vice president.

Jefferson had Burr arrested for treason in 1807. Chief Justice John Marshall presided over Burr's trial. The case against Burr proved weak, and after a thirty-day trial, the former vice president was cleared of all charges in September. Burr moved to Europe for four years, and Jefferson turned his attention to more pressing problems as conflict developed between two US allies, France and Great Britain.

TROUBLE WITH FOREIGN TRADE

Over the course of Jefferson's presidency, US profits from international trade had increased, largely due to military conflicts between Great Britain and France. The United States had maintained neutrality, which allowed US businesses to trade freely with both of the warring nations. The United States' export trade grew too as European trade limitations made American reexports to Europe more desirable. In short, neutrality had proved beneficial to the US economy, and Jefferson hoped to continue this pattern.

PROPOSED PUBLIC WORKS

Early in his second term, Jefferson proposed an amendment that would enable the government to fund "education, roads, rivers, canals, and other such objects of public improvement." In 1808 Treasury secretary Albert Gallatin suggested that $20 million go toward improving the nation's roads and canals. More pressing budgetary concerns prevented his proposal from passing, but in time, most of these projects were indeed carried out. Jefferson's administration was the first to suggest such means of improving the nation's infrastructure.

Albert Gallatin's 1808 Report on Roads, Canals, Harbors, and Rivers proposed that the government pay to build new transportation systems in the expanding country. Until then, private companies built roads and charged fees to users.

However, in 1803, after two years of peace, war again broke out between France and Great Britain. Fueled by the ambitions of the French leader Napoleon, the Napoleonic Wars would last until 1815. During this renewed conflict, the United States was caught in the middle of France and Great Britain's trade restrictions. Despite Jefferson's determination to keep the United States neutral, Britain's Royal Navy often stopped US merchant ships, claiming they were carrying goods destined for enemies of the British. The navy would then seize cargo, men, and even the vessels themselves. To a lesser extent, the French navy harassed US merchant ships too.

British press gangs boarded the American trading ships they stopped to search for deserters from their navy. The press gangs took away anyone unable to prove US citizenship and forced the kidnapped sailors into service in the Royal Navy—a practice called impressment. Of the ten thousand sailors the British impressed, only about one thousand had actually deserted the British navy. Most often they were British-born but naturalized US citizens.

In response, early in 1806, Jefferson asked Congress to pass a law to limit trade between the United States and Great Britain to pressure Britain to stop impressing US sailors. On April 18, Congress passed the Non-Importation Act. This law restricted US merchants from importing British goods that Congress believed could be manufactured in the United States instead. Banned items included beer, playing cards, glass, brass, silver, clothing, and wool.

Thomas Jefferson soon tasked James Monroe and William Pinkney, the ministers to Great Britain, with negotiating a treaty with the British government that would protect US trading vessels and end British impressment of US citizens. In March 1807, Jefferson received a draft of the Monroe-Pinkney Treaty. To his disappointment, the agreement failed to address

British navy officers, such as the two on the right, boarded American trade ships in search of sailors they could force to serve in their own navy.

impressment, and he refused to deliver the treaty to the Senate. Instead, he asked Monroe and Pinkney to revise the treaty's terms, which ultimately proved unsuccessful.

THE *CHESAPEAKE-LEOPARD* INCIDENT

Tension between the United States and Great Britain continued to build. In February of 1807, rumors claimed that three British sailors had deserted the Royal Navy and sought safety aboard the USS *Chesapeake*. Secretary of State Madison looked into the matter and determined that the men in question were US citizens who had previously been impressed by the British navy. Therefore, they were not actual deserters. The Royal Navy, however, ordered captains stationed along the US coast to stop and search the *Chesapeake* if

sighted. On June 22, 1807, the British *Leopard* spotted the *Chesapeake* along the Virginia coast. The *Chesapeake*'s captain refused to allow the British sailors to board. The *Leopard* fired into the American frigate, killing three American sailors and injuring eighteen. The *Chesapeake* then surrendered to the *Leopard*. British sailors boarded the damaged ship and seized the three sought-after men.

Outraged, Jefferson and his administration demanded that the British compensate the US government for its losses. Britain refused even to respond. On July 2, 1807, acting without the consent of Congress, Jefferson ordered all British ships to leave US waters. A few days later, he notified state governors to send militiamen to protect US waters from the British. The nation was in an uproar, as anti-British feeling flared. Jefferson noted, "This country has never been in such a state of excitement since the Battle of Lexington," the battle that had started the American Revolution.

The Leopard (left) *fired on the* Chesapeake *after the captain refused to let the British board and search the ship.*

THE EMBARGO ACT OF 1807

In the midst of the confrontation, Jefferson pondered three options: "War, Embargo, or Nothing shall be the course. The middle proposition is most likely." Many politicians strongly opposed the idea of an embargo to limit trade. James Sullivan, the governor of Massachusetts, argued that an embargo would hurt his state, home to much of America's commercial shipping. Treasury secretary Gallatin also hoped for war instead of an embargo. He explained to Jefferson, "In every point of view, privations, sufferings, revenue, effect on the enemy, politics at home, etc., I prefer war to a permanent embargo."

Nevertheless, Jefferson decided that an embargo was the most prudent choice. To Gallatin he wrote, "What is *good* in this case cannot be [accomplished]; we have, therefore, only to find out what will be *least bad*." He viewed an embargo as a temporary measure that could hold off a war for which the nation was unprepared. It would give time for the United States to build up its military and, Jefferson hoped, for the threat of war to blow over.

Congress passed the Embargo Act of 1807 on December 22. The act prohibited US merchants from trading with Europe. Jefferson intended the embargo to protect American sailors and vessels by keeping them away from British and French ships. The halt in trade would also apply economic pressure to Great Britain and France that would, Jefferson hoped, result in peace.

The embargo struck the United States' economy hard. Profits from US foreign trade plummeted by almost 80 percent, from $108 million in previous years to $22 million by the embargo's end fifteen months later. A surplus of the main export goods—flour, raw cotton, rice, and tobacco—caused prices to drop sharply early in 1808. Meanwhile, the prices of imported goods increased by about one-third. Many people struggled to afford necessities at these higher rates.

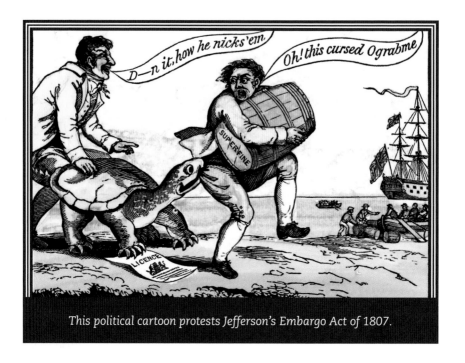

This political cartoon protests Jefferson's Embargo Act of 1807.

US citizens wrote to the president condemning him for the embargo. One man wrote to Jefferson, "You infernal villain. How much longer are you going to keep this . . . Embargo on to starve us poor people. One of my children has already starved to death of which I am ashamed and declared that it died of an apoplexy. I have three more children which I expect will starve soon if I don't get something for them to eat which cannot be had."

The president exercised extraordinary control and authority to enforce the embargo. US merchants began to defy Jefferson's embargo, smuggling goods over the northern border, where they could be shipped out from Canadian ports. To thwart this practice, Jefferson refused to allow merchants to export goods via inland waters as well as overland. When the smuggling continued, he called on the military to enforce the embargo, and he ordered port authorities to confiscate the cargoes of any ships suspected of illegal trade.

The embargo was not working as planned on the international front either. The effects on the French and British economies were not significant enough to spur the countries to change their policies.

Foreign trade profits would not return to preembargo levels until the 1840s. The embargo did increase US domestic manufacturing. New England had opened seven new factories in 1807. One year later, during the height of the embargo, plans in the region were under way to construct twenty-six factories.

James Madison, Jefferson's successor, would face the same problems with the British that Jefferson had, including the impressment of sailors. In 1812 President Madison declared war against Great Britain. The War of 1812 (1812–1815) would take fifteen thousand US lives before a treaty reestablished friendly US-British trade.

Under the Embargo Act, many traders could transport goods only over land instead of by sea.

In 1807 Jefferson could not foresee the embargo's failure, but he was well aware of the precedents that his policies were creating. The Embargo Act of 1807 gave the federal government power to control the economic activities of US citizens. The president's use of the military to enforce the embargo strengthened the control of government even further. Despite his commitment to limited government and rule of the people, Jefferson had violated these principles to take what he saw as the most practical course.

ABOLITION OF THE SLAVE TRADE

One of Jefferson's most significant foreign policy acts came toward the end of his presidency. The constitutional protection of the transatlantic slave trade was due to expire in 1808, and Jefferson wanted Congress to ban the import of slaves into the United States as soon as possible. In his annual message to Congress, on December 2, 1806, he urged the legislative body to "withdraw the citizens of the United States from all further

A slave trade ship taking aboard slaves off the coast of Africa. Ships transported slaves from Africa to the United States.

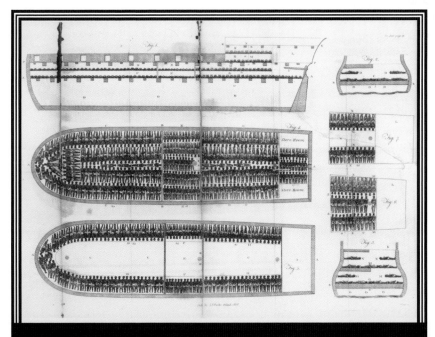

Slave traders transported slaves in their ships' cramped cargo holds. This diagram shows the approximate layout of the ships and the number of slaves that were carried in each one.

participation in those violations of human rights which have been so long continued on the unoffending inhabitants of Africa, and which the morality, the reputation, and the best interests of our country have long been eager to proscribe [outlaw] . . ."

On March 2, 1807, Congress passed a bill that "prohibit[ed] the importation of slaves into any port or place within the jurisdiction of the United States." The following day, Jefferson signed the bill into law. Because of the prior constitutional restriction, the law could not take effect until January 1, 1808.

With the bill's passage, slave traders could no longer bring enslaved people into US ports. Anyone who owned a slave ship or attempted to import slaves from abroad faced large fines and possibly imprisonment. The bill left the internal slave trade intact, however.

"AM I NOT A MAN AND A BROTHER?"

Peter Williams Jr., a Christian minister, was a free African American in New York City in the early nineteenth century. He worked toward equal rights for African Americans and the abolition of slavery. On January 1, 1808, the day the new law against importing slaves took effect, he addressed the congregation of the African Methodist Episcopal Zion Church quoting Jefferson's words.

> When the inspired voice of Americans first uttered those noble sentiments, "we hold these truths to be self-evident, that all men are created equal . . . ;" and when the bleeding African, lifting his fetters, exclaimed, "am I not a man and a brother;" then with redoubled efforts, the angel of humanity strove to restore to the African race, the inherent rights of man.
>
> Rejoice, Oh, ye descendants of Africans! No longer shall the United States of America . . . swell the tide of African misery, by the importation of slaves.

Williams's speech was printed soon afterward as An Oration on the Abolition of the Slave Trade. It is one of the first published works about abolition by an African American.

As a Christian minister, Peter Williams Jr. spoke for the abolition of slavery.

Slave owners could still buy and sell enslaved African Americans within the United States until the Thirteenth Amendment abolished all US slavery in 1865. Furthermore, an illegal international slave trade flourished, with traders smuggling as many as twenty thousand slaves into the United States each year until the close of the American Civil War (1861–1865).

★ CHAPTER SIX ★

AN ACTIVE RETIREMENT

The promise of retirement had tantalized Thomas Jefferson for years. As early as 1807 he had begun to pack up and ship items back to Monticello in preparation for his permanent return in 1809. His decades in the public eye had worn him ragged, and he was eager to embrace a life free from political demands.

As his final days in office drew to a close, Jefferson expressed relief, as well as his optimism for the young nation's future leadership, to his friend Pierre S. du Pont de Nemours. "Never did a prisoner released from his chains feel such relief as I shall on shaking off the shackles of power. Nature intended me for the tranquil pursuits of science, by rendering them my supreme delight," he wrote on March 2. He continued, "I leave everything in the hands of men so able to take care of them, that if we are destined to meet misfortunes, it will be because no human wisdom could avert them."

Thomas Jefferson remained in Washington to see the inauguration of his successor, fellow Democratic-Republican and old friend, James Madison, on March 4, 1809. Within days, the former president returned to Monticello, never to leave Virginia again.

This is a copy of a portrait Thomas Sully painted in 1821, after Jefferson's retirement from politics.

RETIREMENT

Though retired from politics, Jefferson remained intensely busy, pursuing his many interests, such as experimenting with scientific methods of gardening and farming, designing architecture (including endless improvements to Monticello), playing music, and studying religion.

Throughout his life, Jefferson had exchanged letters with friends around the world. Among his correspondents had been John Adams. After more than a decade of silence, the two overcame their political differences and resumed their friendship.

ON THE MOUNTAINTOP

Monticello was Jefferson's haven. Even during his presidency he stayed at his Virginia estate for weeks at a time, conducting his government business by mail.

Jefferson, a skilled amateur architect, designed Monticello based on the style of sixteenth-century Italian architect Andrea Palladio. Jefferson began drawing up plans for the house in 1768 and never stopped remodeling it. In the 1790s, he even ordered the house torn down and completely rebuilt, adding the iconic dome and doubling the size. The larger house helped accommodate frequent houseguests and Jefferson's extensive collections of books and artifacts.

Jefferson designed the three-story Monticello to look like a one-story building.

These collections reflected a lifetime of curiosity, exploration, and love of knowledge. Items from Lewis and Clark's expedition, maps, and art all needed space. Jefferson also designed mechanical gadgets "with a greater eye to convenience." These included a clock that kept track of both the time and the calendar day, a revolving book stand that displayed five books at once, and a rotating clothes rack in the closet.

Jefferson designed Monticello's grounds as well, planning and tending to the hundreds of types of flowers, fruits, and vegetables in the estate's vast gardens. He also oversaw Mulberry Row, a stretch of road that was the center of daily life on the plantation for dozens of enslaved and free people. It included slave quarters, storehouses, and workshops for nail making, weaving, and other industries.

Monticello was not completed until 1809, almost forty years after Jefferson began construction. The house appears on the US nickel coin.

Among Jefferson's many inventions are the writing desk (left) and the rotating book stand (right).

At the start of his reacquaintance with Adams, Jefferson wrote, "A letter from you recalls recollections very dear to my mind. It carries me back to the the times when, beset with difficulties and dangers, we were fellow laborers in the same cause, struggling for what is most valuable to man, his right of self-government." Between 1811 and 1826, Adams and Jefferson exchanged 158 letters on topics ranging from history and philosophy to grief and aging.

UNIVERSITY OF VIRGINIA

A longtime dream of Jefferson's was to start a public university in Virginia. In retirement, he set to work planning his school, which would be built in nearby Charlottesville. Jefferson wrote that he wanted to start a school that would "form the statesmen, legislators and judges, on whom public prosperity

Jefferson designed the Rotunda of the University of Virginia, a building which still stands as the university's central structure.

MONEY PROBLEMS

Thomas Jefferson borrowed huge sums of money throughout his life. Part of the problem stemmed from debt he inherited when John Wayles, his father-in-law, died in 1773. Wayles had been rich in land and slaves but poor in cash. Jefferson's expensive lifestyle further contributed to his lifelong money troubles.

The British army burned the Capitol Building in Washington, DC, during the War of 1812, and with it burned the 3,000 books in the Library of Congress. In 1815 Jefferson sold his library of 6,487 books to the US government to make up the Library of Congress's new collection. Jefferson received $23,950 for the volumes, but this was not nearly enough to pay his creditors. When Jefferson died, he owed more than $100,000 (several million dollars in modern terms). Jefferson's family sold the Monticello plantation and the enslaved African Americans there to pay off his debts.

and individual happiness are so much to depend," and "develop the reasoning faculties of our youth, enlarge their minds, cultivate their morals, and install into them the precepts of virtue and order." Universities had traditionally been associated with religious denominations, but Jefferson planned one of the first based on religious freedom and the separation of church and state.

Jefferson took an active role in the publicly funded school. He planned the course of study, appointed faculty, and designed the campus. Jefferson saw the school doors open to the first students in March 1825. Only white males could attend.

By 1826 eighty-three-year-old Jefferson's health was failing. On July 3, he floated in and out of consciousness, awakening to ask, "Is it the Fourth?" Thomas Jefferson died after noon on July 4, 1826, fifty years to the day since his Declaration of Independence had brought the United States to life.

In Massachusetts, the health of ninety-year-old John Adams had been failing too. Five hours after Jefferson breathed his last, Adams died too. His final words were "Thomas Jefferson survives."

JEFFERSON'S LEGACY

Although Jefferson had died before Adams, the words "Jefferson survives" still ring true. Jefferson's influence and ideals live on. He penned the words that people around the world still recognize as the founding principle of the United States: "We hold these truths to be self-evident: that all men are created equal."

Jefferson's fame as a founder, however, may obscure his real accomplishments as president. Jefferson himself didn't count the presidency among the three accomplishments to be engraved on his gravestone: "Author of the Declaration of Independence and of the Virginia Statute for Religious Freedom, and father of the University of Virginia."

With his faith in the common citizen's ability to govern himself, Jefferson had steered the nation away from the legacy of British royalty and toward a true democracy. His presidency and his Democratic-Republican Party marked the start of a succession of leaders who followed these principles.

Despite Jefferson's personal money troubles, he was a talented administrator of the nation's finances. Together, he and Secretary of the Treasury Gallatin lowered taxes and were still able to decrease the nation's debt by $26 million.

Jefferson's gravestone stands in his family's graveyard at Monticello.

One of the most enduring legacies of Jefferson's presidency was his purchase of the Louisiana Territory from France. For the sum of $15 million, Jefferson almost doubled the size of the young United States. By sponsoring the Corps of Discovery, Jefferson paved the way for US settlement and trade in the West. In addition to making contact with American Indian nations, the corps identified 178 plants and 122 animals previously unknown to European Americans. The expedition allowed the United States to lay claim to the Oregon Territory in the Pacific Northwest, which the nation gained in 1819.

As more Americans moved west, migration routes such as the Santa Fe and Oregon Trails drew thousands of settlers through the former Louisiana Territory. This westward expansion sparked conflicts as new settlers clashed with American Indians who struggled to hold onto their homelands. Jefferson's early policy of purchasing land from American Indians gave way to more sweeping measures to move them off their lands through coercion and force.

A complicated, conflicting legacy on race and slavery trails behind Jefferson, clearly illustrating his struggles to align his ideals and his actions. Despite his iconic words asserting the equality of all people, Jefferson believed that people of African descent were biologically inferior to white people. Jefferson denounced slavery as a moral depravity and played a key role in abolishing the transatlantic slave trade, yet he held more than six hundred slaves during his lifetime, freeing just ten of them.

Lawyer, statesman, author of the Declaration of Independence, diplomat to France, secretary of state, vice president, and president—Jefferson left in his wake a powerful mixture of triumphs and failures that continue

Jefferson passed many substantial pieces of legislature during his presidency. Here he stands beside the Declaration of Independence.

to impact the United States and even the world. His actions as president were just a fraction of what he achieved throughout his lifetime, but they nonetheless profoundly shaped the course of American history.

Depictions of Jefferson's likeness can be found on the nickel; on the two-dollar bill; on Mount Rushmore; and at the Jefferson Memorial in Washington, DC. These tributes are symbols of Jefferson's contributions. But even without these physical reminders of his influence, Jefferson survives, as does his lifelong, complicated quest to ensure the rights "to life, liberty, and the pursuit of happiness."

TIMELINE

1743: Thomas Jefferson is born in Albemarle County in Virginia.

1757: Jefferson's father dies.

1767: After studying law under George Wythe, Jefferson is admitted to the Virginia bar to practice law.

1768: Thomas Jefferson is elected into the Virginia House of Burgesses.

1772: Jefferson and Martha Wayles Skelton marry.

1774: *A Summary View of the Rights of British America* is published. This gains Jefferson recognition as an American patriot leader.

1775: Thomas Jefferson is selected to attend the Second Continental Congress.

1776: Jefferson, along with Benjamin Franklin, Robert Livingston, John Adams, and Roger Sherman, pens the Declaration of Independence. The members of the Continental Congress approves the document on July 4.

1777: Jefferson drafts the Virginia Statute for Religious freedom. It passes in 1786.

1782: Martha Wayles Skelton Jefferson, Thomas's wife, dies after a difficult childbirth.

1789: President George Washington appoints Jefferson as the nation's first secretary of state.

1797: Jefferson becomes vice president to John Adams.

1801: Jefferson is inaugurated as the third president of the United States.

1803: The United States pays $15 million for the Louisiana Territory.

1804: The Corps of Discovery, led by Meriwether Lewis and William Clark, departs from Saint Louis, Missouri.

1807: Congress, pressed by Jefferson, passes the Embargo Act of 1807.

1809: Construction is completed on Monticello.

1825: The University of Virginia, founded by Jefferson, opens its doors to its first students.

1826: Thomas Jefferson dies at Monticello on July 4, fifty years to the day after the signing of the Declaration of Independence.

SOURCE NOTES

6   Margaret Bayard Smith, *The First Forty Years of Washington Society,*
    ed. Gaillard Hunt (New York: Charles Scribner's Sons, 1906), 26,
    http://babel.hathitrust.org/cgi/pt?id=mdp.39015027775694;view=1
    up;seq=11.

7   "Physical Descriptions of Jefferson," *Thomas Jefferson Encyclopedia,*
    accessed November 3, 2015, https://www.monticello.org/site
    /research-and-collections/physical-descriptions-jefferson.

8   Thomas Jefferson, "First Inaugural Address," Avalon Project,
    accessed November 3, 2015, http://avalon.law.yale.edu/19th
    _century/jefinau1.asp.

8   Thomas Jefferson, *The Life and Selected Writings of Thomas Jefferson,*
    ed. Adrienne Koch and William Peden (New York: Modern Library,
    1998), 298.

8   Jefferson, "First Inaugural Address."

11 "Jefferson's College Life," William & Mary, accessed December 15,
    2015, http://www.wm.edu/about/history/tjcollege/tjcollegelife
    /index.php.

15 R. B. Bernstein, *Thomas Jefferson* (New York: Oxford University
    Press, 2003), 31.

17 "The Declaration of Independence: A Transcription," National
    Archives, accessed January 4, 2016, http://www.archives.gov
    /exhibits/charters/declaration_transcript.html.

18 "Thomas Jefferson and the Virginia Statute for Religious
    Freedom," Virginia Historical Society, accessed October 27, 2015,
    http://www.vahistorical.org/collections-and-resources/virginia
    -history-explorer/thomas-jefferson.

18 "Thomas Jefferson and Slavery," *Thomas Jefferson Encyclopedia,*
    accessed October 27, 2014, http://www.monticello.org/site
    /plantation-and-slavery/thomas-jefferson-and-slavery.

19 Jon Meacham, *Thomas Jefferson: The Art of Power* (New York:
    Random House, 2012), 142.

20   Meacham, *Thomas Jefferson*, 476.

21   "Martha Wayles Skelton Jefferson," *Thomas Jefferson Encyclopedia*,
      accessed October 28, 2015, https://www.monticello
      .org/site/jefferson/martha-wayles-skelton-jefferson.

23   Thomas Jefferson, "To James Madison Paris, Dec. 20, 1787,"
      American History, accessed November 20, 2015, http://www
      .let.rug.nl/usa/presidents/thomas-jefferson/letters-of-thomas
      -jefferson/jefl66.php.

27   Bernstein, *Thomas Jefferson*, 117.

28   John Ferling, "Thomas Jefferson, Aaron Burr and the Election of
      1800," *Smithsonian Magazine*, November 1, 2004, http://www
      .smithsonianmag.com/history/thomas-jefferson-aaron-burr-and
      -the-election-of-1800-131082359/?no-ist.

30   Jefferson, *The Life and Selected Writings*, 298–299.

31   Thomas Jefferson, "Letter to Spencer Roane," September 6, 1819,
      The Founder's Constitution, accessed December 20, 2015, http://
      press-pubs.uchicago.edu/founders/documents/a1_8_18s16.html.

31   Meacham, *Thomas Jefferson*, 363.

36   "An Act in Addition to the Act, Entitled 'An Act for the
      Punishment of Certain Crimes against the United States,'" Avalon
      Project, accessed October 30, 2014, http://avalon.law.yale
      .edu/18th_century/sedact.asp.

37   Ibid.

41   "Marbury v. Madison (1803)," FindLaw, accessed November 17,
      2014, http://caselaw.lp.findlaw.com/scripts/getcase.pl?navby
      =case&court=us&vol=5&page=137.

42   Bernstein, *Thomas Jefferson*, 151.

45   Gerard W. Gawalt, "America and the Barbary Pirates: An
      International Battle against an Unconventional Foe," The Thomas
      Jefferson Papers, American Memory from the Library of Congress,
      accessed October 25, 2014, http://memory.loc.gov/ammem
      /collections/jefferson_papers/mtjprece.html.

46   Anthony Brandt, "Tripoli Pirates Foiled," *Military History* 28, no. 4
      (November 2011): 42.

46 "The Marines' Hymn," Marines, accessed November 20, 2015, http://www.hqmc.marines.mil/hrom/NewEmployees /AbouttheMarineCorps/Hymn.aspx.

47 Joseph J. Ellis, *American Sphinx: The Character of Thomas Jefferson* (New York: Knopf, 1998), 241.

47 "The First Barbary War," *Thomas Jefferson Encyclopedia*, accessed October 22, 2014, http://www.monticello.org/site/research-and -collections/first-barbary-war.

50 "The Louisiana Purchase," *Thomas Jefferson Encyclopedia*, accessed October 26, 2014, http://www.monticello.org/site /jefferson/louisiana-purchase.

50 Fawn M. Brodie, *Thomas Jefferson: An Intimate History* (New York: W. W. Norton, 1974), 341.

51 Meacham, *Thomas Jefferson*, 387.

53 Thomas Jefferson, "Jefferson to James Monroe, July 14, 1793," *Thomas Jefferson Encyclopedia*, accessed December 4, 2015, https:// www.monticello.org/site/research-and-collections/st-domingue -haiti.

54 Meacham, *Thomas Jefferson*, 387.

54 Ibid.

55 "Letter to John C. Breckinridge," August 12, 1803, TeachingAmericanHistory.org, accessed November 3, 2014, http:// teachingamericanhistory.org/library/document/letter-to-john-c -breckinridge/.

56 Thomas Jefferson, "Jefferson's Confidential Letter to Congress," Monticello.org, accessed October 22, 2014, http://www.monticello .org/site/jefferson/jeffersons-confidential-letter-to-congress.

58 Ibid.

60 Thomas Jefferson, "Jefferson's Instructions to Meriwether Lewis," Monticello.org, accessed October 29, 2014, http://www.monticello .org/site/jefferson/jeffersons-instructions-to-meriwether-lewis.

61 "Sacagawea," PBS, accessed December 20, 2015, http://www.pbs .org/lewisandclark/inside/saca.html.

61 "Jean Baptiste Charbonneau," *PBS*, accessed December 20, 2015, http://www.pbs.org/lewisandclark/inside/jchar.html.

63 "Corps of Discovery," *The West, PBS*, accessed December 20, 2015, http://www.pbs.org/weta/thewest/program/episodes/one/corpsof.htm.

66 Thomas Jefferson, "Sixth Annual Message to Congress, December 2, 1806," Avalon Project, accessed November 6, 2014, http://avalon.law.yale.edu/19th_century/jeffmes6.asp.

69 Jefferson, "Sixth Annual Message to Congress."

72 "Embargo of 1807," *Thomas Jefferson Encyclopedia*, accessed December 20, 2015, http://www.monticello.org/site/research-and-collections/embargo-1807.

73 Meacham, *Thomas Jefferson*, 428.

73 Ibid.

73 Ibid.

74 Ibid.

77 Thomas Jefferson, "Sixth Annual Message (December 2, 1806)," Miller Center, University of Virginia, accessed October 24, 2014, http://millercenter.org/president/jefferson/speeches/speech-3495.

77 "An Act to Prohibit the Importation of Slaves into Any Port or Place within the Jurisdiction of the United States," Avalon Project, accessed November 4, 2015, http://avalon.law.yale.edu/19th_century/sl004.asp.

78 Peter Williams Jr., "An Oration on the Abolition of the Slave Trade; Delivered in the African Church in the City of New-York, January 1, 1808," ed. Paul Royster, University of Nebraska–Lincoln, accessed January 4, 2016, http://digitalcommons.unl.edu/etas/16.

80 Thomas Jefferson, "To P. S. Dupont de Nemours Washington, March 2, 1809," American History, accessed November 30, 2015, http://www.let.rug.nl/usa/presidents/thomas-jefferson/letters-of-thomas-jefferson/jefl192.php.

83 "I Rise with the Sun," Monticello.org, accessed November 30, 2015, https://www.monticello.org/site/jefferson/i-rise-sun.

84   Meacham, *Thomas Jefferson*, 457.

85   Ibid.

85   Bernstein, *Thomas Jefferson*, 174.

86   Meacham, *Thomas Jefferson*, 493.

86   Ibid.

86   "John Adams," Monticello.org, accessed February 24, 2016, https://www.monticello.org/site/jefferson/john-adams.

86   Bernstein, *Thomas Jefferson*, ix.

89   Meacham, *Thomas Jefferson*, 104.

GLOSSARY

corsair: a pirate, especially along North Africa's Barbary Coast

Democratic-Republican Party: a political party that believed in a strict interpretation of the Constitution and strong state government rather than federal government. The Democratic-Republican Party emerged in the 1790s. It dissolved in 1825 and is not related to the present-day Democratic Party or the Republican Party.

Electoral College: a body of voters that elects a president and vice president

embargo: an official government order that does not allow trading vessels to leave port

Federalist Party: a political party that believed in a loose interpretation of the Constitution and a strong central government. The Federalist Party formed in the 1790s and had disappeared by the 1820s.

impressment: the forcible seizure of men for service in the military

mercenary: a soldier who accepts payment to fight for another country

Northwest Passage: a water route Jefferson and others hoped existed between the Missouri River and the Pacific Ocean

pardon: to officially declare that a person convicted of a crime is no longer considered guilty

partisan: a person who is intensely loyal to a party, group, or person

pasha: an official of high rank, from the Ottoman (Turkish) Empire

press gang: a group of men that physically forced others to serve in the British military

ratify: to approve or confirm

reexports: foreign goods shipped into US ports and then repackaged for export

right of deposit: the freedom to temporarily store goods before they are loaded onto oceangoing merchant ships for export

tribute: money given to another country in exchange for protection from harm

writ of mandamus: a formal legal document that orders a person to perform an official duty

SELECTED BIBLIOGRAPHY

Appleby, Joyce. *Thomas Jefferson*. New York: Times Books, 2003.

Bernstein, R. B. *Thomas Jefferson*. New York: Oxford University Press, 2003.

Brodie, Fawn M. *Thomas Jefferson: An Intimate History*. New York: W. W. Norton, 1974.

Jefferson, Thomas. *The Life and Selected Writings of Thomas Jefferson*. Edited by Adrienne Koch and William Peden. New York: Modern Library, 1998.

Meacham, Jon. *Thomas Jefferson: The Art of Power*. New York: Random House, 2012.

Peterson, Merrill D. *Thomas Jefferson and the New Nation*. New York: Oxford University Press, 1970.

Thomas Jefferson Encyclopedia. Monticello.org. Accessed February 22, 2016. http://www.monticello.org/site/research-and-collections/tje.

FURTHER INFORMATION

Anderson, Michael, ed. *Thomas Jefferson*. New York: Britannica, 2013.
Learn more about the details of this founder's personal and
political life.

Drive, Stephanie Schwartz. *Understanding the Declaration of Independence*.
New York: Rosen, 2011.
Discover more about this cornerstone document of the United States,
primarily written by Jefferson.

Hollar, Sherman, ed. *Biographies of the New American Nation: George
Washington, Thomas Jefferson, Frederick Douglass, and More*. New York:
Britannica, 2013.
Learn about visionaries from Jefferson's time and the impact they had on
the formation of the young United States.

January, Brendan. *The Aftermath of the Wars against the Barbary Pirates*.
Minneapolis: Twenty-First Century Books, 2009.
Find out how the lessons the United States learned in the Barbary Wars
helped it approach future military conflicts.

Jefferson, Thomas. "Autobiography, 1743–1790," Bibliomania
http://www.bibliomania.com/2/9/63/110/20912/1/frameset.html
In 1821, at the age of seventy-seven, Jefferson wrote these recollections
of his life. He covers his family history and the founding of the United
States, and ends at the time he became secretary of state.

The Monticello Classroom
http://classroom.monticello.org/kids/home
Check out this wealth of Jefferson-related resources and images to learn
more about the life and times of the third president.

Moore, Kathryn. *The American President: A Complete History*. New York: Fall
River, 2007.
This comprehensive volume offers fascinating details about each
president and presidency.

Stanton, Lucia. *"Those Who Labor for My Happiness": Slavery at Thomas Jefferson's Monticello*. Charlottesville: University of Virginia Press, 2012. This book sheds light on Jefferson as a slaveholder and the lives of the enslaved individuals at Jefferson's plantation, Monticello.

Thomas Jefferson Papers, Massachusetts Historical Society
http://www.masshist.org/thomasjeffersonpapers
This site presents digital images of Jefferson's original papers, along with information about them. They include Jefferson's handwritten *Notes on the State of Virginia* and his architectural drawings and garden notebooks.

White House—Thomas Jefferson
http://www.whitehouse.gov/about/presidents/thomasjefferson
Read up on Jefferson at the White House's official website.

INDEX

PHOTO ACKNOWLEDGMENTS

The images in this book are used with the permission of: © Universal History Archive/UIG via Getty Images, pp. 1, 2 (handwriting); Gift of Thomas Jefferson Coolidge IV in memory of his great-grandfather, Thomas Jefferson Coolidge, his grandfather, Thomas Jefferson Coolidge II, and his father, Thomas Jefferson Coolidge III, Image courtesy of the Board of Trustees, National Gallery of Art, Washington DC, p. 2 (portrait); © iStockphoto.com/hudiemm, (sunburst); © iStockphoto.com/Nic_Taylor (parchment); Design Pics/Newscom, p. 3 (signature); © iStockphoto.com/ Phil Cardamone, p. 3 (bunting); The Granger Collection, New York, pp. 6, 11, 40, 76; Albert and Shirley Small Special Collections Library, University of Virginia, p. 9; © North Wind Picture Archives/Alamy, pp. 12, 51, 74, 75; © Kentucky Gateway Museum Center, Maysville, Kentucky, p. 13; © Arthur Ackermann Ltd., London/Bridgeman Images, p. 14; Library of Congress, pp. 15, 17, 32, 45, 53, 77, 88; Architect of the Capitol, p. 16; © Tony Fischer/ Wikimedia Commons (CC BY 2.0), p. 18; © Virginia Historical Society, Richmond, Virginia, USA/Bridgeman Images, p. 19; © Everett Collection Historical/Alamy, p. 21; © National Portrait Gallery, Washington DC, USA/Photo © GraphicaArtis/Bridgeman Images, p. 22 (left); Ailsa Mellon Bruce Fund, Image courtesy of the Board of Trustees, National Gallery of Art, Washington DC, pp. 22 (right), 54; © Glasshouse Images/ Alamy, p. 24; The Miriam and Ira D. Wallach Division of Art, Prints and Photographs: Print Collection, The New York Public Library, Astor, Lenox and Tilden Foundations, pp. 25, 33; Gift of Mrs. Robert Homans, Image courtesy of the Board of Trustees, National Gallery of Art, Washington DC, p. 28; © American Antiquarian Society, Worcester, Massachusetts, USA/Bridgeman Images, p. 29; © National Portrait Gallery, Smithsonian Institution/Art Resource, NY, p. 34; © Everett Historical/Shutterstock. com, p. 35; Wikimedia Commons, p. 36; © PAUL J. RICHARDS/AFP/Getty Images, p. 39; © Niday Picture Library/Alamy, p. 41; Gift of John P. Lyman/ New Hampshire Historical Society, p. 42; © US Naval Academy Museum, Annapolis, Maryland/Wikimedia Commons, pp. 46, 48; © Internet Archive Book Images/Wikimedia Commons, p. 47; © Peter Newark American Pictures/Bridgeman Images, pp. 49, 64, 67, 68; Samuel H. Kress Collection, Image courtesy of the Board of Trustees, National Gallery of Art, Washington DC, p. 50; © Bibliotheque Nationale, Paris, France/Bridgeman Images, p. 52; © Bob Wick/BLM/flickr.com (CC BY 2.0), p. 57; Independence National Historical Park, p. 59; Lewis and Clarke at Three Forks by E. S. Paxson, Mural at the Montana State Capitol, Oil on canvas, 1912, Courtesy of the Montana Historical Society, X1912.07.01, p. 61; TOM GRALISH/KRT/ Newscom, p. 63; © Collection of the New-York Historical Society, USA/

ABOUT THE AUTHOR

Emily Rose Oachs graduated with a degree in communication studies. She works as a freelance writer and editor and has authored more than thirty nonfiction books for children and young adults. She lives in Los Angeles.